THE LITTLE
BOOK OF
DIRTY
JOKES

THE LITTLE BOOK OF DIRTY JOKES

First published in 2012 as *Really Blokey Jokes*

This revised edition copyright © Summersdale Publishers Ltd, 2015

Illustrations © Shutterstock

Summersdale Publishers Ltd
46 West Street
Chichester
West Sussex
PO19 1RP
UK

www.summersdale.com

Printed and bound in the Czech Republic

ISBN: 978-1-84953-785-8

Substantial discounts on bulk quantities of Summersdale books are available to corporations, professional associations and other organisations. For details contact Nicky Douglas by telephone: +44 (0) 1243 756902, fax: +44 (0) 1243 786300 or email: nicky@summersdale.com.

THE LITTLE BOOK OF

DIRTY JOKES

Sid Finch

summersdale

Why is sex like a game of bridge?

If you don't have a good partner, you'd better have a good hand.

Three old ladies were resting their aching joints on a park bench when a man jumped out from behind a bush, flashed them and ran off.

Two of them had a stroke, but the third was too slow.

How did the armless man do in the wanking competition?

He came nowhere.

....

What do you call a man who can crawl along the floor without using his arms or legs?

Clever dick.

A teenage couple are feeling horny and go back to the boy's house for a steamy night of passion. Before they go upstairs, the boy says to the girl, 'By the way, I still share a room with my little brother but he won't see us because I sleep on the top bunk. We'll have to whisper to each other in code though, so if you want me to go faster say "bread" and if you want me to slow down say "butter".' The girl agrees and they get into bed and start going for it, with the girl calling out 'bread' and then 'butter' every few minutes. Just as the boy climaxes, his little brother calls out, 'Can you two go and make your sandwiches in the kitchen? You're getting mayonnaise all over me!'

A man and woman had been married for 30 years, and in those 30 years, they always left the lights off when having sex. He was embarrassed and scared that he couldn't please her, so he always used a big dildo on her. All these years, she had had no clue. One day, she decided to reach over and flip the light switch on and saw that he was using a dildo. She said, 'I knew it, asshole; explain the dildo!' He shouted back, 'Explain the kids!'

What do train sets and boobs have in common?

Both were designed for kids, but it's always dads who end up playing with them.

A woman walks into a chemist and asks if they sell extra-large condoms. 'Yes, we do,' says the sales assistant. 'Would you like to buy some?'

'No thanks,' replies the woman. 'But if you don't mind, I'll wait here for someone who does.'

A man goes to the doctor for his annual check-up, and the doctor tells him, 'You need to stop masturbating.'

The man asks, 'Why?'

The doctor replies, 'Because I'm trying to examine you.'

An American college graduate was travelling in Europe and met a beautiful blonde Swedish girl. He asked her out, and while they were dancing, he put his arms around her and said, 'In America, we call this a hug.' She replied, 'Yaah, we are also calling it a hug in Sveden.' So far so good, he thought, and decided to try for a French kiss. He said, 'In the States, we call this a kiss.' She replied, 'Yaah, in Sveden also, this is a kiss.' They had a couple more drinks and then he suggested they go outside. Finding a nice quiet spot in a nearby park, he undressed her and they started to have sex. He said, 'In America, we call this a grass sandwich.' She replied, 'Yaah, in Sveden we call it a grass sandwich too, but usually we are putting more meat in it.'

What's the definition
of trust?

Getting a blow job
from a cannibal.

....

What do tofu and a
dildo have in common?

They're both meat
substitutes.

A woman went to see her gynaecologist and complained of a sore vagina. During the examination, the doctor found a small vibrator stuck inside her. 'Ah,' he said, 'I think I can see what's causing your discomfort, but I'm afraid that removing the, er... obstruction requires a lengthy, delicate and expensive surgical operation.' 'Well,' said the woman, 'I don't think I can afford it right now. As I'm here though, could you replace the batteries?'

**A bloke tells a girl
in a bar that he
has six willies.**

**'What a load of
bollocks!' she replies.**

Why does the Incontinence Hotline need so many people working the phones?

Because the callers can never hold.

Two teenagers are making out. The girl asks the boy if he wants to try a 69. 'What's that?' asks the boy. 'Well,' the girl explains, 'I put my head between your legs while you put yours between mine.' Without fully understanding what she means, but not wanting to spoil his chances, the boy agrees and they undress. Just as they get into position, the girl farts. The boy struggles free and jumps off the bed in disgust. The girl, embarrassed, apologises and promises it won't happen again. They move into position again, but straight away the girl lets out another stinker. Utterly revolted, the boy leaps up and begins to dress. 'What's going on? You're not leaving, are you?' asks the girl. The boy replies, 'Do you really think I'm going to hang around for the other 67?'

What do a great
boyfriend and a bottle
of Glenfiddich 50 Year
Old have in common?

They're both
good lickers.

A man enters a pharmacy, buys a packet of condoms and leaves the shop laughing hysterically. The pharmacist finds this a bit strange but shrugs it off – after all, the guy may be a bit strange, but there's no law to prevent strange people from buying condoms and it would be a good story to tell the wife later.

The next day the man comes back, buys another packet of condoms and leaves the pharmacy in hysterics once again. Intrigued, the pharmacist calls his assistant over and says to him, 'If that bloke ever comes back, I want you to follow him to see where he goes.' Sure enough, on the following day he's back and repeats the performance. This time, the assistant follows him. An hour later, the assistant returns. 'So! What was he doing?' the pharmacist asks. 'Uh, well...' the assistant hesitates. 'I followed him to your house...'

A man on a train is eating prawns, throwing the shells out of the window. An old lady sitting opposite him says, 'Could you stop doing that please? It's disgusting!' He replies, 'Listen darling, I've paid for my ticket so I'll do what I want on this train!' and continues eating his prawns. Once he's finished he settles down for some shut-eye. Meanwhile, the lady gets her knitting out. Kept awake by the incessant clicking, the man sits up and says, 'Hey Granny! Can you stop that noise? I'm trying to sleep!' 'Listen sweetie,' she replies, 'I also paid for my ticket and I'll do what I want!' Livid, the man stands up, grabs the needles and chucks them out the window. The old lady gets up and pulls the alarm signal. He laughs at her; 'You will get a fine for that!' She sneers back at him, 'And YOU will get ten years when the police smell your fingers!'

What does an 80-year-old woman have between her cleavage that a 25-year-old woman doesn't?

Her belly button.

A man walks into a pub and starts downing shot after shot of whisky. Concerned, the landlord asks if he's alright. 'Not really,' sighs the man. 'I just found my wife in bed with my best friend.' 'Oh dear,' says the landlord, 'What did you say to her?' The man shakes his head and says 'Nothing'. 'So what did you say to your best friend?' The man replies, 'I said, "Bad dog! VERY bad dog!"'

Did you hear about the constipated mathematician?

He worked it out with a pencil.

At a tribal coming-of-age ceremony, a youth is placed in front of three tents. The chief of the tribe says to him, 'In the first tent there is a barrel of plum wine: you must drink it all. In the second tent there is a puma with a raging toothache: you must take out the bad tooth.

And in the third tent awaits a woman who has never had an orgasm...' The young man enters the first tent and comes back out of it rather quickly, holding the empty barrel and looking somewhat worse for wear. The tribe applauds him. He bumbles into the second tent. The tribe holds its breath as terrible screams, yowls and growls issue forth from the tent. Just when everyone begins to think the young man must be dead he emerges, exhausted and bloody, and says, 'Now lead me to the woman with the toothache!'

A bloke checking into a hotel asks at reception whether the porn channel in his room is disabled.

'No,' the receptionist replies, 'it's just regular porn.'

One day Jane decided to give Tarzan some sex education. 'Look, Tarzan, the thing you have between your legs is like your laundry. And what is between my own legs is like a washing machine. So, all you have to do is put your laundry into my washing machine and squeeze it well before taking it out.' For the following five nights, Tarzan did the washing non-stop. When he finally stopped for a break, Jane said to him, 'Listen, Tarzan, you can't keep doing the laundry constantly – you're going to wear out my washing machine! You'll have to wait for two or three days before doing your next load.' Tarzan was very disappointed at this. After a month of no laundry, Jane asked him, 'Tarzan, what's wrong with you? Why haven't you put your laundry into my machine for a month?' Tarzan replied, 'Tarzan handwash!'

Two inflatable sex dolls are walking through the desert.

Suddenly, the first doll shouts out to the second one, 'Watch out for the CACTUSSSSSSsssssss...'

What do you get
when you cross a
rooster and an owl?

A cock that stays
up all night.

A traditional dairy farmer decides that it's time to move with the times, and invests in an automatic milking machine. On the day it arrives, his wife is away at market and he can't resist the temptation to try it out on himself. After a frustrating hour spent setting the thing up, he finally gets it working, sticks the sucking teat on to the end of his cock and switches it to the highest setting. He quickly experiences an explosive orgasm, but when it's all over he finds he can't disengage from the machine. Panicking, he dials the customer service number on the packaging and says, 'Hello, I have just purchased one of your milking machines. It all seems to be in working order, but I can't seem to find the release mechanism.' 'Not to worry, Sir,' comes the reply, 'the machine will automatically disengage once it has extracted two gallons.'

A sex-shop sales assistant picked up a call from a distressed customer, who said, 'Heello, I boouugghht aaaa vviibbrrattorr ffrroomm yourrrrr sshhopppp a fffffew daaays aggggooo.'

The assistant replied, 'Oh yes, how can I help?'

'Ccaann yyoouu tteell mmee hhooww ttoo ttuurrnn tthee ffuucckkiinngg tthhiinngg oofff?'

Two Americans were in a London museum admiring a well-endowed male statue.

One says to the other, 'No, I think Big Ben is a clock, dear.'

A woman walks into
a bar and asks for a
'double entendre'...

... so the barman
gives her one.

Sarah was comforting her 99-year-old grandmother after the death of her grandfather, and asked how he had died. Sobbing, her grandmother replied, 'He had a heart attack while we were making love last Sunday.' Shocked, Sarah said, 'Goodness, Granny! Having sex at your age, weren't you just asking for trouble?' 'No, no, darling,' said the grandmother, 'when we both started getting on a bit, we decided only ever to make love when the church bells were ringing — that way we could keep to a nice steady rhythm. You know: in on the "ding", out on the "dong"... and if it wasn't for that bloody ice-cream van, he'd still be alive today!'

What three words would be the worst to hear while having sex?

'Honey, I'm home.'

....

What's the best advice for first-time sex-toy purchasers?

Think long and hard when buying a dildo.

A female police officer pulls
a man over for drink-driving
and decides to arrest him.

'Anything you say can and will be
held against you,' says the officer.

'BREASTS!' shouts the man.

Why is Viagra good for old men?

It stops them rolling out of bed.

....

What's the difference between eggs and a blow job?

You can beat eggs, but you can't beat a blow job.

A bloke goes to a fancy-dress party in only his underwear.

'What are you meant to be?' asks the host.

'A premature ejaculation!' the bloke replies. 'I just came in my pants.'

Two little boys are sitting next to each other in Sunday school. One little boy says to the other, 'Which part of the body goes to heaven first?' His friend replies, 'Oh, it's definitely the legs.' 'How do you know that?' asks the first boy. 'Well,' says the second boy, 'I've seen Mummy on her back, waving her legs in the air and screaming, "Oh God, I'm coming!"'

Why didn't the John Wayne toilet paper work?

It won't take shit off anyone.

Three blokes went on a camping holiday together and were sharing a tent. After their first night, the man on the right-hand side of the tent said, 'I had a really vivid dream last night, that a sexy girl was tossing me off.' 'That's weird,' said the man on the left-hand side of the tent, 'I dreamt the same thing.' The man in the middle sat up and said, 'Sounds better than my dream – I dreamt I went skiing...'

What's grey and comes in pints?

An elephant.

....

What's the difference between a G spot and a golf ball?

Men will spend time looking for a golf ball.

What did the man do with the dog that kept licking his balls?

Take it home.

....

Why are vegetarians good at head?

Because they've had lots of practice eating nuts.

What's worse than lobsters on your piano?

Crabs on your organ.

....

What's the difference between a Christmas bonus and your boner?

It's easy to blow your own bonus.

A psychiatrist was conducting a group therapy session with three young mothers and their small children. 'You all have obsessions,' he observed. To the first mother, he said, 'You are obsessed with eating. You've even named your daughter Candy.' He turned to the second mom. 'Your obsession is money. Again, it manifests itself in your child's name, Penny.' At this point, the third mother got up, took her little boy by the hand and whispered, 'Come on, Dick, let's go.'

A promiscuous girl goes to the dry cleaners to clean a blouse.

'Can you get the stain off?' she mumbled.

'Come again?' asks the attendant.

'No, just coffee this time.'

Mr Bear and Mr Rabbit live in the same forest, but they don't like each other. One day, they come across a golden frog who offers them three wishes each. Mr Bear wishes that all the other bears in the forest were female. Mr Rabbit wishes for a crash helmet. Mr Bear's second wish is that all the bears in the neighbouring forests were female as well. Mr Rabbit wishes for a motorcycle. Mr Bear's final wish is that all the other bears in the world were female, leaving him the only male bear in the world. Mr Rabbit revs the engine of his motorcycle and says, 'I wish that Mr Bear was gay!' and rides off.

There were two eggs boiling in a pan. One egg said to the other, 'Oh look, I've got a crack.'

The other replied, 'Well there's no point telling me: I'm not hard yet!'

Two blokes walking down the street catch sight of a dog lying down licking its own balls. One says to the other, 'Don't you wish you could do that?'

The other bloke replies, 'Nah. He'd probably try to bite me.'

A woman was bored at home while her husband was away on business and decided to visit a fortune teller who had travelled to the area. The fortune teller immediately guessed that this woman was sexually frustrated and produced a jar which contained a pickled penis. 'If you want a good time,' she explained, 'all you have to do is unscrew the lid and say, "Pickled penis: my vagina".' The woman paid up and took the penis home.

That night she gave it a try and found that it worked, with fantastic results. She was moaning with pleasure when her husband arrived home, banged on the bedroom door and demanded to know who she had in there with her. 'It's OK, darling,' she said, 'It's just my pickled penis.' As he burst through the door, her husband shouted, 'Pickled penis my ass!'

What's the difference between a rectal and an oral thermometer?

The taste.

....

What do you call two scotch bonnets having sex?

Fucking hot!

A family is at the dinner table. The son asks the father, 'Dad, how many kinds of boobs are there?' The father, surprised, answers, 'Well, son, a woman goes through three phases. In her twenties, a woman's breasts are like melons: round and firm. In her thirties and forties, they are like pears: still nice, but hanging a bit. After fifty, they are like onions.' 'Onions?' the son asks. 'Yes. You see them and they make you cry.' This infuriated his wife and daughter. The daughter asks, 'Mom, how many different kinds of willies are there?' The mother smiles and says, 'Well, dear, a man goes through three phases also. In his twenties, his willy is like an oak tree: mighty and hard. In his thirties and forties, it's like a birch: flexible but reliable. After his fifties, it's like a Christmas tree.' 'A Christmas tree?' the daughter asks. 'Yes: dead from the root up and the balls are just for decoration.'

It was a chilly winter night and two bulls were shivering in the farmer's field. One bull said to the other, 'Gosh it's cold!'

'Yes, it is,' agreed the other bull. 'You know, I might just go and slip into a nice Jersey.'

Three guys compare their levels of intoxication from a party the previous night. The first guy says, 'Man, I was so drunk last night, I went home and blew chunks.' The second guy says, 'I was so drunk last night, I woke up this morning on my front porch.' The third guy says, 'I was so drunk last night, I had sex with three strange women.' The first guy exclaims, 'You guys don't understand! Chunks is my dog!'

A rugby player is lying in hospital after a debilitating kick to the groin. 'Are my testicles black?' he mumbles to the nurse through his oxygen mask. She raises his gown, cups his penis in one hand, feels his balls with the other and takes a close look. After her inspection she says, 'They seem to be fine.' The man removes his mask and says, 'Well, thanks for that — it was quite something! But what I really wanted to know is... are my test results back?'

Why are sperms shaped like tadpoles?

Because frogs are too hard to swallow.

....

What do you call someone who refuses to fart in public?

A private tutor.

A little old lady is late for mass and settles into a pew just as the priest is saying, '... and everyone who has recently committed adultery should stand up.' Being somewhat hard of hearing, she asks her neighbour to repeat what the priest has just said. 'He said everyone who wants a mint should stand up.' The old lady unsteadily gets to her feet, much to the priest's horror. He exclaims, 'At your age? You should be ashamed!' The old lady swiftly retorts, 'Just because I don't have any teeth left, doesn't mean I can't suck on something from time to time!'

Which animal can change sex in less than a second?

The crab.

....

One football player boasted to another, 'I've fucked a Brazilian.'

The other player replied, 'That's amazing! How many is a Brazilian?'

A man gets into a lift and finds himself alone with a beautiful woman. After a short time he looks her way and asks, 'Excuse me for asking, but can I smell your fanny?'

Disgusted and indignant, the woman replies, 'You certainly cannot!'

'Oh,' says the man, 'it must be your feet then.'

A gorgeous woman is house-sitting for friends and decides to take a bath. As she slips into the water, the doorbell rings, but she can't find a towel so she calls out, 'Who's there?' and hears the response, 'It's the blind man.' Thinking how lucky that is, she opens the door without bothering to cover herself up. 'Great boobs, love,' says the man. 'Now, where are those broken blinds?'

Two mates were out for a pint and the conversation soon turned to sex. 'So, do you ever do it doggy style with your girlfriend?' said one to another. 'Not really,' his friend replied, 'I'd say she's more into dog tricks than doggy style.' 'Oh, so she's pretty kinky then?' asked the first man, winking. 'Well, not exactly,' explained his friend. 'I sit up and beg and she rolls over and plays dead!'

What do westerns and porn films have in common?

The heroes never need to reload.

What's the difference between 'Oooh!' and 'Aaah!'?

About three inches.

....

How do you test an archaeologist?

Give him a used tampon and ask him what period it came from.

Two sperm are in the body looking for the egg when one of them starts to wonder why it is taking so long.

He asks the other sperm, 'Aren't we near the uterus yet?'

'No,' replied the other sperm, 'we haven't even reached the oesophagus.'

Two police officers are walking the beat when one says, 'When I get home, I'm going straight upstairs and tearing off the wife's underwear.'

'Feeling randy?' asks the other.

'No,' says the first. 'The elastic is killing me.'

A man sees a sign outside a bar that reads '£10 for a good time'. Unable to resist this offer, he goes in and pays up. The bartender leads the man to a back room where he finds himself alone with a sheep. Thinking he might as well get his money's worth, he has his way with the sheep and leaves. The next week he returns and this time sees a sign which boasts, '£20 for the time of your life!' He pays up, but this time is taken upstairs to another room, where he finds a group of men staring through a crack in the floor. He peeks through and sees two people having sex. Impressed, he turns and gives the thumbs up to the bloke next to him, who says, 'Last week was even better; some pervert was shagging a sheep!'

The local mayor was visiting a hospital where several new wards had opened. On her guided tour of the hospital, she hears orgasmic moans coming from a room down the corridor. Overcome with curiosity, she slips away and goes into the room to investigate. There she finds a man openly masturbating on the bed. She calls to a nurse and asks why he's doing that, and the nurse replies, 'He suffers from a rare condition which makes him need to relieve himself regularly.' Slightly revolted but determined not to appear fazed, the mayor continues her tour, only to hear more orgasmic noises from another room further along. This time she goes into the room to find a nurse giving a patient a blow job. Somewhat alarmed, she asks her escort what's going on. The nurse replies, 'This man has the same disorder as the man you saw in the previous room, but this one has private health insurance.'

An old man goes to his doctor and says, 'Can you give me something to lower my sex drive?'

The doctor replies, 'I would have thought at your age it's all in the mind.'

'It is,' agrees the old man. 'That's why I want it lower.'

Two 90-year-olds had been dating for a while when the man said to the woman, 'Well, tonight's the night we have sex!' And so they did. As they lay next to each other in bed afterwards, the man turned to the woman and said, 'If I'd known you were a virgin, I'd have been much more gentle.'

The woman replied, 'Well if I'd known you'd actually manage to get it up, I'd have taken my knickers off!'

A cucumber is chatting to an olive and a penis, and says to them, 'My life is so depressing. When I get big, fat and juicy they're going to slice me up and put me in salad.' The olive says, 'It's worse for me: when I get big, fat and juicy they'll chop me into bits and sprinkle me on a pizza.' The penis says, 'I can top that! When I get big, fat and juicy, they stick a bag over my head, shove me down a narrow tunnel and leave me there till I throw up.'

Why is an umbrella like a cock?

You have to get it up to use it, it comes down when you're done and dribbles after use.

Two ducks go away together for a dirty weekend. However, when they arrive at their hotel room, they realise they've forgotten to bring any condoms, so the male duck calls room service and asks for one to be sent up. Moments later, there's a knock at the door. The male duck opens the door to find a man with a condom on a tray. He takes the condom, puts a tip on the tray and says thank you. Before he leaves, the man asks, 'Sir, would you like me to put that on your bill?' 'Good lord no!' quacks the duck in shock. 'Do you think I'm some sort of pervert?!'

Teacher: Use the word 'contagious' in a sentence.

Student: My neighbour is building a garage all by himself. My dad says it will take the contagious.

Why do beavers swim
on their backs?

To keep their nuts dry.

....

A doctor is examining
a woman: Ma'am, you
have acute angina.

Woman: Why, thank
you doctor!

A couple are celebrating their twenty-fifth wedding anniversary and have returned to the hotel where they spent their honeymoon. As they reminisce about their first night together, the wife asks the husband, 'Darling, what were you thinking the first time you saw me standing naked in front of you?' The husband replies, 'I was just thinking how much I wanted to shag your brains out, and suck your tits dry.' Feeling horny, the wife begins to undress and asks cheekily, 'And what are you thinking right now?' Surveying her body he replies, 'I'm thinking that it looks as if I did a pretty good job.'

What do you get if you mix an aphrodisiac and a laxative?

Easy come, easy go.

....

What do you call a dickhead sitting in a tree with a briefcase?

A branch manager.

A man had always dreamt of having a pair of real cowboy boots. One day he sees a pair on sale, decides to treat himself and walks proudly back home in his new boots. He enters the house and asks his wife, 'Do you notice anything different about me?' The wife looks him up and down and says that she doesn't. Frustrated, the husband locks himself in the bathroom, takes off his clothes and comes back completely naked but still wearing his cowboy boots. He says to his wife, 'And NOW do you notice something different?' The wife looks at him again and says, 'What's different darling? It droops today, drooped yesterday and it will still be drooping tomorrow...' Furious, the husband cries out, 'And do you know why? It's drooping because it's admiring my new cowboy boots!' The wife thinks for a moment and replies, 'So maybe you should buy a new hat!'

A chicken is lying in bed next to an egg, smoking a cigarette and grinning.

The egg, looking annoyed, says, 'Well, I guess we answered that question!'

A couple head back to the man's flat after a date. As the man gets his key out the woman says, 'Did you know you can judge a lover by the way he unlocks a door?' 'Is that true? How?' asks the man. 'Well,' says the woman, 'For example, if a man sticks the key straight in and barges through the door, that means he's rough in bed, which I don't like. And if it takes him ages to get the key in the slot, he's inexperienced, which I don't like either.' Then she asks him, 'So, what's your approach?' The man replies, 'Well, before I even try to put my key in, I give the lock a good licking.'

A farmer is sitting in the kitchen when his son comes in from the barn with a large glass of white liquid.

'Look dad! I just milked the cow!'

Then he takes a big drink from the glass. His father just stares at him.

'Son, we don't have a cow. We have a bull.'

An ugly bloke enters a bar and is soon surrounded by women. Another man asks him his secret.

The ugly bloke shrugs and says, 'All I did was start licking my eyebrows.'

A woman finds an
S&M magazine under
her son's bed, so
she goes to speak
to her husband.

'What shall we
do?' she asks.

'Well, whatever you
do, don't spank him,'
replies her husband.

A doctor complains to his colleagues about the sanitary problems at a badly run latex glove factory. 'Workers stick their hands in melted latex and then dip their hands in a vat of cooling water to solidify the latex. The glove is then thrown in a finished products box.' His colleagues are disgusted by the lack of care taken in keeping the gloves sanitary. 'That's not all,' says the doctor. 'You don't even want to know how they make their condoms!'

How can you spot
a blind man in a
nudist colony?

It's not hard.

....

What are the four
greatest kings
in history?

Licking, sucking,
wanking and fucking.

If you think your life is bad, imagine being an egg:

you only get laid once, you only get smashed once and the only woman to sit on your face is your mother.

It's a really hot day and a penguin is having car trouble, so he takes it into a garage. The penguin asks, 'How long will it be?' The mechanic says, 'Just a few minutes.' So the penguin decides to go and get an ice cream at the grocery store across the street. When the penguin gets there he climbs inside the big freezer door and starts to eat ice cream. Three hours go by before the penguin looks at his watch and jumps out of the freezer and races back to the garage. With ice cream all over his face and his stomach he says, 'So, how's my car?' The mechanic comes walking out wiping his hands on a rag and says, 'Looks like you blew a seal.' The penguin says, 'No, no, no, I was just eating ice cream.'

A husband and wife are trying to set up a new password for their computer. The husband types in 'Mypenis'.

The wife falls on the ground laughing: on the screen it says, 'Error. Not long enough.'

What did Adam say to Eve?

'Stand back! I don't know how big this thing gets!'

....

What do you get if a donkey eats an overweight male chicken?

A fat cock in the ass.

Condoms are not completely safe.

A friend of mine was wearing one and he got hit by a bus.

A woman says to her best friend, 'My husband and I have what he calls Olympic sex.'

Her friend replies, 'Wow, that must be a terrific sex life!'

The woman sighs sadly and says, 'Not really. It only happens once every four years.'

A man says to a woman, 'Am I the first man you ever made love to?'

She replies, 'You might be. Now you come to mention it, your face does look familiar.'

A man walks into a bar and says, 'C-c-can I h-have a b-b-beer?' The bartender replies, 'Of course. You know, I used to stutter myself, but one afternoon my wife gave me three blow jobs in a row, and I haven't stuttered since!' The man says, 'Th-th-thanks, th-th-that's g-g-great adv-v-v-ice...' A week later, the man returns and once again asks, 'C-c-can I h-have a b-b-beer?' Curious, the bartender asks whether the man tried his stutter cure. 'Oh, I d-d-did!' says the man, 'It j-j-just d-d-didn't w-w-work. B-b-but I m-m-must say, your w-w-wife g-gives g-g-g-gr-great h-h-head!'

John was showing off his new sports car to his girlfriend. 'If I can get up to 200 mph, will you strip off?' he asked. 'OK!' she agreed. He revved the engine and before long the car was speeding along at 200 mph. True to her word, his girlfriend got completely naked. John couldn't keep his eyes on the road, and the car skidded on to a grassy verge and flipped over. His naked girlfriend was thrown out of the car and landed unscathed, but John was trapped beneath the steering wheel. 'Get help!' he shouted. 'But I haven't got any clothes on and the doors are jammed shut!' She replied. 'Here, take my shoe to cover yourself,' said John. With the shoe held over her pubes, the girl ran to the nearest petrol station and said to the attendant, 'You have to help me – my boyfriend's stuck!' Looking at the shoe, the pump assistant said, 'I don't think there's anything I can do – looks like he's in too far.'

Two nuns are driving through
the woods at night.
Suddenly, Satan appears before them
and starts to mount the car.
One of the nuns says to the other, 'Sister
Mary, quickly show him your cross!'
So Sister Mary winds down the window,
sticks out her head and shouts,
'GET THE FUCK OFF MY CAR BONNET!'

52 THINGS TO DO WHILE
YOU POO

Hugh Jassburn

ISBN: 978-1-84953-497-0

Hardback

£6.99

Perching on the porcelain can be very boring
when you have nothing to do but poo. But
fear no more, as excretion expert Hugh
Jassburn has put together a compendium
of entertaining activities and informative
fun that will make you want to stay put,
even if you don't need to go. Doing a
number two will never be the same again.

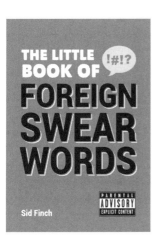

THE LITTLE BOOK OF
FOREIGN SWEAR WORDS

Sid Finch

ISBN: 978-1-84953-771-1

Paperback

£5.99

Ever been lost for words
in a foreign country?

When you want to get your point across
abroad, there's only one way to do it: by
swearing your ar*e off! Impress the world
with a stream of multilingual profanity
from this nifty little book.

If you're interested in finding out more about our books, find us on Facebook at **Summersdale Publishers** and follow us on Twitter at **@Summersdale**.

www.summersdale.com